THE BOSTON RED SOX

BY

MARK STEWART

Content Consultant
James L. Gates, Jr.
Library Director
National Baseball Hall of Fame and Museum

NORWOOD HOUSE PRESS

CHICAGO, ILLINOIS

Norwood House Press
P.O. Box 316598
Chicago, Illinois 60631

For information regarding Norwood House Press, please visit our website at:
www.norwoodhousepress.com or call 866-565-2900.

All photos courtesy of AP Images—AP/Wide World Photos, Inc. except the following:
The Fan Craze Company (6); F.W. Rueckheim & Brother (7 & 16 right);
Black Book archives (8, 22, 23 top, 28, 35 top right, 37 bottom, 38 & 41 right);
Topps, Inc. (9, 21 bottom, 31 right, 35 top left and bottom left, 37 top & 40 top and bottom);
Bowman Gum, Inc. (14); Recruit (16 left); Golden Press (20); Gum, Inc. (21 top);
Exhibit Supply Company (34 top); Author's collection (34 left & 41 top);
Sports Stars Publishing (43).
Special thanks to Topps, Inc.

Editor: Mike Kennedy
Designer: Ron Jaffe
Project Management: Black Book Partners, LLC.
Special thanks to Steve Krasner

Library of Congress Cataloging-in-Publication Data

Stewart, Mark, 1960-
  The Boston Red Sox / by Mark Stewart ; with content consultant James L.
Gates, Jr.
      p. cm. -- (Team spirit)
  Summary: "Presents the history, accomplishments and key personalities of
the Boston Red Sox baseball team. Includes timelines, quotes, maps, glossary
and website"--Provided by publisher.
  Includes bibliographical references and index.
  ISBN-13: 978-1-59953-059-8 (library ed. : alk. paper)
  ISBN-10: 1-59953-059-7 (library ed. : alk. paper)
  1. Boston Red Sox (Baseball team)--History--Juvenile literature. I.
Gates, Jr., James L. II. Title. III. Series: Stewart, Mark, 1960- Team
spirit.
  GV875.B62S74 2007
  796.357'640974461--dc22
                                        2006015489

Manufactured in the United States of America.

COVER PHOTO: The Red Sox celebrate the final out of their 2004 championship.

Table of Contents

SPORTS WORDS & VOCABULARY WORDS: In this book, you will find many words that are new to you. You may also see familiar words used in new ways. The glossary on page 46 gives the meanings of baseball words, as well as "everyday" words that have special baseball meanings. These words appear in **bold type** throughout the book. The glossary on page 47 gives the meanings of vocabulary words that are not related to baseball. They appear in ***bold italic type*** throughout the book.

Meet the
Red Sox

When a baseball player agrees to play for a team, he really is little more than an *employee*. When a player pulls on the uniform of the Boston Red Sox, he becomes part of something much bigger. The Red Sox are a baseball "family" with roots that go back more than a *century*. The family members include players past and present, the fans in the stands, and millions of people throughout New England who root for the team.

Like most families, the Red Sox have gone through happy times and sad times. Sometimes they have gotten along with one another, and sometimes they have not. In the end, however, all of these experiences have drawn them closer together.

This book tells the story of the Red Sox. They have had some of the game's greatest teams and players. They also have been a part of baseball's most exciting moments. When you go to a Red Sox game, there is always a chance that you will see something you will never forget.

Pitchers Josh Beckett and Curt Schilling watch their teammates and talk a little baseball.

Way Back When

The story of the Red Sox begins more than a century ago, when the **American League (A.L.)** formed in 1901. Boston already had a **National League (N.L.)** team, but it was not doing very well. The owners in the new league thought they could steal their fans away. The new team was called the Americans, then the *Puritans*, and then the Pilgrims. Finally, in 1907, they became the Red Sox.

By that time, the Red Sox had already won the **pennant** twice. They finished atop the A.L. in 1903 and beat the Pittsburgh Pirates in the first modern **World Series**. They won the pennant again in 1904, but no World Series was played. The team's early stars included Buck Freeman, Jimmy Collins and Cy Young. Young was baseball's most famous pitcher.

Between 1912 and 1918, the Red Sox won four pennants and four World Series. These teams were among the greatest in history. Boston's incredible pitching staff included Joe Wood, Rube Foster, Ernie Shore, Dutch Leonard, Carl Mays, Joe Bush, and Babe Ruth. Tris Speaker, Harry

Buck Freeman and Jimmy Collins, the hitting stars of the 1903 and 1904 team.

SPEAKER, Boston - Americans

Center fielder Tris Speaker, who led the Red Sox to the championship in 1912 and 1915.

Hooper, Larry Gardner, and Duffy Lewis were the hitting stars.

In 1918, the Red Sox decided that Ruth was too good a hitter to be a full-time pitcher, and began playing him in the outfield. He led the league in home runs that season, and also won 13 games on the mound. In 1919, Ruth set a new record with 29 home runs—quite a feat in the days when ballparks were very large and baseballs did not travel as far as they do today.

After the season, the team's owner, Harry Frazee, sold Ruth to the New York Yankees for $100,000. Some believe he decided to use the money to put on a play instead of spending it to improve the team. The play made money, but the team started to lose. During the 1920s and 1930s, the Red Sox often finished in last place.

Their luck began to change at the end of the 1930s, when they traded for slugger Jimmie Foxx and pitcher Lefty Grove. Then a great young hitter named Ted Williams joined the team. The Red Sox added Bobby Doerr, Johnny Pesky, and Dom DiMaggio, and won the pennant in 1946. However, they lost the World Series in seven games. More good players joined the team—including Ellis

Kinder, Mel Parnell, and Jackie Jensen—but Boston did not capture another pennant until 1967.

That season, the Red Sox won a four-way battle for first place in the American League. They were led by manager Dick Williams and young stars Carl Yastrzemski and Jim Lonborg. However, Boston lost the World Series in seven games. In 1975, Yastrzemski was joined by All-Stars Carlton Fisk, Jim Rice, Fred Lynn, and Luis Tiant. The Red Sox reached the World Series once more, but again they lost in seven games.

In 1986, the Boston team led by Roger Clemens, Wade Boggs, and Rice came within one out of winning the championship. Their opponents in the World Series, the New York Mets, made an amazing comeback and beat the Red Sox in—what else?—seven games. Boston fans were heartbroken. Some feared that they would never win the World Series. It would be 18 long years before they would get another chance.

TOP: Carl Yastrzemski, who starred for the Red Sox from 1960 to 1983.
LEFT: Roger Clemens, Boston's greatest pitcher.

The Team Today

Every time the Red Sox fell short of a championship, the more *frustrated* the fans and players became. In 2003, the team was just a few outs away from the pennant, but lost to the New York Yankees. With the pressure to win becoming almost **unbearable**, the players made a decision—they would just relax, have fun, and really enjoy baseball for a change.

Led by hitters David Ortiz, Manny Ramirez, and Johnny Damon, and pitchers Curt Schilling and Pedro Martinez, the 2004 Red Sox had a great year. They won 98 games, and then defeated the Anaheim Angels and New York Yankees in the **playoffs** to win the pennant. In the World Series, they beat the St. Louis Cardinals, sweeping all four games.

Today the Red Sox no longer think about the 86 years it took to win a championship. They think about playing hard and having fun. They are good enough to win the championship every year, and confident enough to make it happen again.

Wily Mo Pena, Manny Ramirez, and
Trot Nixon celebrate another Boston victory.

Home Turf

The Red Sox play their home games in Fenway Park. It is the oldest stadium in the major leagues, and it has not changed much over the years. A trip to Fenway gives you a good idea of how "cozy" ball parks were a century ago. Some of the stadium's seats are closer to home plate than the dugouts.

Because Fenway Park had to fit inside a rectangular city block, right field and center field are far from home plate. Left field, on the other hand, is very close. To make it harder to hit home runs, the Red Sox built the wall very high. It is nicknamed the "Green Monster." A few years ago, the team decided to construct seats on top of the "Green Monster." They have become the most popular seats in Fenway Park.

FENWAY PARK BY THE NUMBERS

- *There are 36,298 seats in Fenway Park.*
- *The left field wall is 37 feet high.*
- *The stadium was built in 1912.*
- *The distance from home plate to the left field foul pole is 310 feet.*
- *The distance from home plate to the center field fence is 420 feet.*
- *The distance from home plate to the right field foul pole is 302 feet.*

Fenway Park's "Green Monster" as seen from the rightfield corner.

Dressed for Success

Baseball teams in Boston had been wearing red socks long before the Red Sox came to town. The city's National League team, which won several championships during the 1800s, had actually been called the Red Stockings for many years. The Red Sox borrowed and then shortened this name after their rivals stopped wearing red socks in 1907. Before that, the Red Sox had blue uniforms.

The first true Red Sox uniform not only included red socks, it actually had a picture of a red sock across the uniform top. In the 1930s, the team started using the fancy "B" on its cap, as well as the blue and red combination it has today.

The Red Sox have changed the style of their uniform from time to time, but over the last 70 years, the basic look has remained the same. The home jersey has "Red Sox" spelled out in fancy lettering, while the darker road jersey has the name of the city.

The 1950s uniform worn here by Walter "Bat" Masterson is almost identical to the one the Red Sox wear today.

UNIFORM BASICS

The baseball uniform has not changed much since the Red Sox began playing. It has four main parts:

- a cap or batting helmet with a sun visor;
- a top with a player's number on the back;
- pants that reach down between the ankle and the knee;
- stirrup-style socks.

The uniform top sometimes has a player's name on the back. The team's name, city, or *logo* is usually on the front. Baseball teams wear light-colored uniforms when they play at home, and darker styles when they play on the road.

For more than 100 years, baseball uniforms were made of wool *flannel* and were very baggy. This helped the sweat *evaporate* and gave players the freedom to move around. Today's uniforms are made of *synthetic* fabrics that stretch with players and keep them dry and cool.

Jason Varitek launches a long drive to right field during the 2006 season. He is wearing his pants high to show his red socks.

We Won!

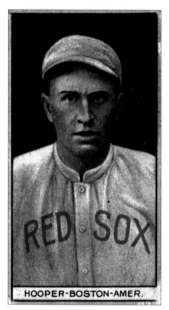

·HOOPER·BOSTON·AMER.·

In October of 1903, the A.L. and N.L. pennant-winners agreed to play for the championship of baseball. This was the first modern World Series. Boston was known as the Pilgrims back then. Very few people thought they could beat the Pittsburgh Pirates, who had Honus Wagner, the best player in the sport.

The first team to win five games would be crowned champions of baseball. Pittsburgh won three of the first four games, but the Pilgrims swept the next four to win five games to three. Boston's pitching was the difference. Cy Young and Bill Dineen had all five of Boston's victories. The Pilgrims' hitting stars were Chick Stahl and Hobe Ferris.

The Red Sox reached the World Series four more times in the early part of the 20th century, and won it each time. Boston beat the New York Giants in 1912, four games to three (with one tie). It was the only one of the World Series that

WOOD, Boston - Americans

was close. Boston won the rest easily. They lost just one game to the Philadelphia Phillies in 1915, and one game to the Brooklyn Robins in 1916. The Chicago Cubs put up a good fight in 1918, but the Red Sox won four games to two.

The Red Sox had many heroes during these victories, including Joe Wood, Tris Speaker, Duffy Lewis, Rube Foster, Ernie Shore, Harry Hooper, Carl Mays, and Babe Ruth. In 1918, Ruth pitched and played the outfield for Boston. He won 13 games, and also led the A.L. in home runs and **slugging average**. In the World Series he beat the Cubs 1–0 and 3–2.

The Red Sox had bad luck in their next four trips to the World Series. Each time—1946, 1967, 1975, and 1986—they lost four games to three. These were some of the most exciting World Series ever played. Boston fans were proud of the Red Sox, but after more than 80 years without a championship, they began to wonder if the team would ever win again.

LEFT: Harry Hooper and Joe Wood, key players in Boston's early pennants. **ABOVE**: Joe Foy watches as Jim Lonborg delivers a pitch in the 1967 World Series. The Red Sox lost to the Cardinals in seven games.

In 2004, Boston made the playoffs as a **Wild Card** team. The Red Sox swept the Angels in the first round, but lost the first three games to the Yankees in the **American League Championship Series (ALCS)**. Led by the heavy hitting of David Ortiz, the team fought back to win the next two games in extra innings.

The famous blood-soaked sock of Curt Schilling. "K ALS" stands for "Strike Out Amyotrophic Lateral Sclerosis"—a cause that is dear to Schilling's heart.

The Red Sox sent Curt Schilling to the mound for the sixth game of the series. Schilling had hurt his ankle in Game One, and was not expected to play again. He agreed to have a special operation that temporarily fixed the injury, so he could pitch one more time. Schilling quieted the Yankee bats as his wound oozed blood through his sock. The Red Sox won 4–2, and beat the Yankees again the next night to win the pennant.

Now all that stood between the Red Sox and a championship were the powerful St. Louis Cardinals. In the first game of the

David Ortiz raises his arms in victory after another
game-winning hit in the 2004 playoffs.

World Series, Boston outscored St. Louis 11–9. After that, the Red
Sox pitchers took over. Schilling threw another great game to win
6–2. Then Pedro Martinez beat the Cardinals 4–1. In Game Four,
Derek Lowe, Bronson Arroyo, Alan Embree, and Keith Foulke
worked together to **shut out** St. Louis 3–0. After 86 years of
disappointment, the Red Sox were champions again.

Go-To Guys

To be a true star in baseball, you need more than a quick bat and a strong arm. You have to be a "go-to guy"—someone the manager wants on the pitcher's mound or in the batter's box when it matters most. Red Sox fans have had a lot to cheer about over the years, including these great stars...

THE PIONEERS

TRIS SPEAKER   Outfielder

• BORN: 4/4/1888   • DIED: 12/8/1958   • PLAYED FOR TEAM: 1907 TO 1915

There may never have been a better center fielder than Tris Speaker. He was a marvelous defensive player, a great hitter, and a swift base-runner.

JIMMY FOXX
first base

JIMMIE FOXX   First Baseman

• BORN: 10/22/1907   • DIED: 7/21/1967
• PLAYED FOR TEAM: 1936 TO 1942

Many experts believe that Jimmie Foxx was the best right-handed power hitter in history. He was nicknamed the "Beast." Foxx hit 50 home runs and won the A.L. batting championship in 1938.

BOBBY DOERR   Second Baseman

• BORN: 4/7/1918   • PLAYED FOR TEAM: 1937 TO 1951

Bobby Doerr was an **All-Star** nine times for the Red Sox. He was a dangerous hitter with men on base, and a very good fielder.

TED WILLIAMS   Outfielder

• BORN: 8/30/1918
• DIED: 7/5/2002
• PLAYED FOR TEAM: 1939 TO 1942 & 1946 TO 1960

Ted Williams understood more about hitting a baseball than any player in history. He won his first batting championship when he was 23 and his sixth when he was 40. Williams was the last player to bat over .400 in a season. In the final at bat of his career, he said farewell to Boston fans with a long home run.

CARL YASTRZEMSKI   Outfielder

• BORN: 8/22/1939
• PLAYED FOR TEAM: 1961 TO 1983

Carl Yastrzemski was Boston's most popular baseball player. At one time or another, he led the A.L. in hits, runs, doubles, home runs, walks, slugging average, batting average, and **runs batted in (RBIs)**. In 1967, "Yaz" won the **triple crown** and almost singlehandedly led the Red Sox to the pennant.

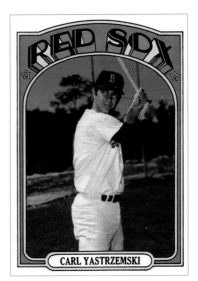

LEFT: Jimmie Foxx   **ABOVE**: Bobby Doerr   **RIGHT**: Carl Yastrzemski

CARLTON FISK   Catcher

- BORN: 12/26/1947   • PLAYED FOR TEAM: 1969 TO 1980

Carlton Fisk was one of the most valuable players in baseball during the 1970s. He controlled the pace of games as a catcher, and was an excellent hitter. His 12th-inning home run in Game Six of the 1975 World Series is one of baseball's most famous moments.

WADE BOGGS   Third Baseman

- BORN: 6/15/1958   • PLAYED FOR TEAM: 1982 TO 1992

Wade Boggs was a hitting machine. Between 1983 and 1988, he won five batting champion-ships. Pitchers hated to throw Boggs a strike—he received the most **intentional walks** in the league six years in a row.

ROGER CLEMENS   Pitcher

- BORN: 8/4/1962   • PLAYED FOR TEAM: 1984 TO 1996

Roger Clemens was the best pitcher in baseball when he played for the Red Sox. He threw three different fastballs and two different **breaking balls**, and he threw them all hard. Clemens was the A.L. **Most Valuable Player (MVP)** in 1986, and won the **Cy Young Award** three times while pitching for Boston.

ABOVE: Wade Boggs   **TOP RIGHT**: Pedro Martinez
BOTTOM RIGHT: David Ortiz and Manny Ramirez

PEDRO MARTINEZ   Pitcher

- BORN: 10/25/1971 • PLAYED FOR TEAM: 1998 TO 2004

Pedro Martinez was a magician with the baseball during his years with the Red Sox. He could throw more pitches at more speeds—and throw them for strikes—than anyone in the game.

MANNY RAMIREZ   Outfielder

- BORN: 5/30/1972 • FIRST YEAR WITH TEAM: 2001

When Manny Ramirez joined the Red Sox, he quickly showed why he was the league's top right-handed hitter. He won the batting championship in 2002 and led the A.L. in home runs in 2004.

DAVID ORTIZ   Designated Hitter

- BORN: 11/18/1975

- FIRST YEAR WITH TEAM: 2003

No one has more fun playing baseball than David Ortiz. He became Boston's dugout leader on their way to the World Series in 2004, and led the league in RBIs in 2005.

On the Sidelines

Many Red Sox managers came and went during the 86 years between Boston's 1918 and 2004 world championships. The team's most famous manager was Joe Cronin. He led the Red Sox from 1935 to 1947, and was also the shortstop for six of those years. Under Cronin, Boston finished second four times, and won the pennant in 1946. He later became president of the American League.

There were other good managers in the Boston dugout over the years, including Dick Williams, Darrell Johnson, Don Zimmer, John McNamara, and Jimy Williams. But not until Terry Francona arrived in 2004 did the Red Sox gain the confidence they needed to win the World Series. Francona was known as a "player's manager." He understood the pressure on major leaguers, and he did his best to help them relax.

Francona became a Boston hero when he led the team to its long-awaited championship in his first year with the team.

Manager Terry Francona keeps his eye on Trot Nixon.

One Great Day

Ted Williams was baseball's most confident hitter. Every time he walked to the plate, he believed he would win his battle with the pitcher and hit the ball hard. In 1941, Williams had a magical season. Yet, for most of the year, no one noticed that his average was over .400. Joe DiMaggio of the Yankees was making headlines every day, getting at least one hit in a record 56 games in a row. Only later that summer did fans realize Williams had a chance to make history, too.

It had been more than 10 years since anyone had batted .400 during a season. Most experts believed it would never be done again. On the season's final day, Williams' average stood at .39955. If he sat out the doubleheader, the league would "round up" this number and credit him with a .400 average. If he played, he risked seeing his average drop. Boston's manager, Joe Cronin, asked Williams what he wanted to do. Williams wanted to "earn" his .400 average. "I'm not going to do it sitting on the bench," he told Cronin.

The Red Sox were playing the Athletics in Philadelphia's Shibe Park. Williams drilled a single his first time up, then hit a home

Ted Williams crosses the plate after a home run in the 1941 All-Star Game. It was a magical season for the "Splendid Splinter."

run. He ended up with four hits in the first game. Williams played in the second game, even though it was difficult to see the ball in the autumn shadows. After hitting a single in his first **at bat**, he hit a pitch in the fourth inning harder than any in his career. The ball went through the infield on a low line, and continued straight to the outfield fence. It hit a speaker and bounced back on the field for a double.

At the end of the day Williams had six hits in eight trips to the plate. He finished the season batting .406. As all those experts predicted, no one has hit .400 since.

Legend Has It

Why was Wade Boggs called the "Chicken Man?"

LEGEND HAS IT that he ate chicken before every game. Like many baseball players, Boggs was superstitious. When he was hitting well, he did not like to change anything he did before a game. Boggs started eating chicken every day as a rookie and hit .349—and never stopped. He hit over .300 for the next nine seasons. To keep from getting bored with chicken, he began trying different recipes. Boggs ended up with so many that he wrote a cookbook called *Fowl Tips*.

ABOVE: Wade Boggs   **RIGHT**: Manny Ramirez and Trot Nixon, two of the stars in Boston's great comeback.

What was the strangest uniform number ever requested by a Red Sox player?

LEGEND HAS IT that it was number 337. One spring in the early 1970s, pitcher Bill Lee asked if he could change his number from 37 to 337. This was not the first unusual thing he had done. In fact, Lee was nicknamed the "Spaceman" because sometimes no one was sure where his mind was. In this case, however, he had a perfectly good reason for the odd request—when you turn 337 upside down, it spells "LEE."

Who made the greatest comeback in playoff history?

LEGEND HAS IT that the 2004 Red Sox did. That year, Boston lost the first three games of the American League Championship Series to the New York Yankees. They were losing Game Four 4–3 in the bottom of the ninth inning. The Red Sox tied the game and won it in the 12th inning. They went on to win the final three games of the series, too. No team in baseball history had ever come back from so far.

It Really Happened

The Red Sox lost the 1975 World Series to the Cincinnati Reds four games to three, but you would never know it talking to Boston's baseball fans. They still rave about Game Six of that series—the most exciting World Series game ever played.

After five games, the Reds held a three games to two lead. When the series moved from Cincinnati to Boston, rain delayed the sixth game for four days. The long wait added to the *drama* of the game, and a record 70 million fans tuned in to watch it on television.

The Red Sox took a 3–0 lead on a home run by Fred Lynn, but the Reds tied the score. Cincinnati scored three more times to take a 6–3 lead. With two outs in the eighth inning, the Red Sox sent **pinch-hitter** Bernie Carbo up to bat. He cracked a long home run with two runners on base to tie the game.

The Red Sox loaded the bases in the next inning, but George Foster made a perfect throw from left field to keep the winning run from scoring. In the 11th inning, Cincinnati's Joe Morgan hit a ball toward the seats in right field, but Dwight Evans caught it before it went over the fence. Who would the next hero be?

His name was Carlton Fisk, and he was one of Boston's most beloved players. Fisk was the leadoff batter in the bottom of the

ABOVE: Carlton Fisk leaps into the air after his home run sails out of the park.   **RIGHT**: An autographed picture of the Boston hero.

12th inning. He swung hard at the first pitch he saw and sent a long, curving drive down the left field line. Everyone in Fenway Park held their breath. Would it go foul? Fisk tried to "help" the ball stay fair by waving his arms. When it curled into the **foul pole**, he jumped for joy. It was a game-winning home run!

Team Spirit

The Red Sox may have a "B" for Boston on their caps, but they are the "home team" for all of New England—including Massachusetts, Rhode Island, Maine, Vermont, New Hampshire, and much of Connecticut. The players on the team today are *celebrities* wherever they travel in the region. Past stars are treated like *royalty*.

The patience and support shown by Boston fans has never been equaled. Many generations of fans rooted for the Red Sox without seeing them win a World Series. The wonderful 2004 championship was their reward.

Another way the team said thanks to its fans was by adding seats atop the "Green Monster." The left field wall in Fenway Park is one of America's most famous "monuments." The chance to watch a game from a seat there is the dream of millions of baseball fans.

Many believed the Red Sox were the victims of a "curse" caused by selling Babe Ruth to the Yankees. These fans celebrate the end of the curse, as the Red Sox close in on their 2004 championship.

Timeline

Dom DiMaggio, the defensive star of the 1946 Red Sox.

1903
The "Pilgrims" defeat the Pittsburgh Pirates in the first modern World Series.

1941
Ted Williams becomes baseball's last .400 hitter.

1946
The Red Sox win the A.L. pennant, but lose to the St. Louis Cardinals in the World Series.

A scorecard from the 1903 World Series.

1918
The Red Sox win their fifth World Series.

1960
Ted Williams hits a home run in the final at bat of his career.

Ted Williams is congratulated after the final home run of his career.

Fred Lynn

Manny Ramirez

1975
Rookie of the Year Fred Lynn wins the MVP award and leads the Red Sox to the World Series.

2002
Manny Ramirez leads the A.L. with a .349 batting average.

1967
Jim Lonborg and Carl Yastrzemski lead the Red Sox to the A.L. pennant.

1986
Roger Clemens strikes out 20 Seattle Mariners in a game.

2004
The Red Sox beat the Cardinals to win their first championship since 1918.

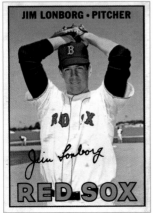

Jim Lonborg

The Red Sox celebrate their 2004 championship.

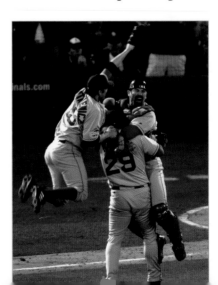

Fun Facts

I DO

In 1998, Boston shortstop Nomar Garciaparra met soccer player Mia Hamm at a penalty kick contest. In 2003, the two stars were married.

FLYING HIGH

Ted Williams missed all or part of five seasons during World War II and the Korean War. With his quick reflexes and excellent eyesight, he was one of America's best fighter pilots.

LOAFING AROUND

Carl Yastrzemski was such a hero to the kids of New England that he had his own brand of white bread: Yaz Bread.

ANYTHING'S POSSIBLE

From 1960 to 1966, the Red Sox never finished higher than sixth place. In 1967, the team shocked the baseball world by winning the A.L. pennant. Fans still call that season "The Impossible Dream."

THE KID CAN HIT

In 1965, Red Sox outfielder Tony Conigliaro led the A.L. in home runs. At the age of 20, he was the youngest player in league history to do so.

YOUNG LEADER

In 1975, Fred Lynn had the greatest year of any Red Sox rookie. He batted .331, led the A.L. in runs and doubles, and helped Boston reach the World Series. After the season, Lynn became the first player ever to be named Rookie of the Year and MVP at the same time.

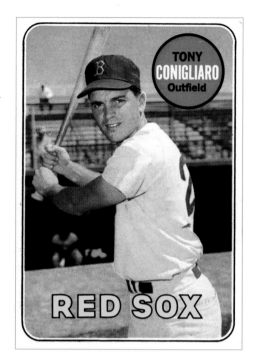

WHAT AN IDIOT!

The 2004 Red Sox were a goofy, fun-loving bunch that called themselves the "Idiots." The "head idiot" was outfielder Johnny Damon.

LEFT: Mia Hamm and Nomar Garciaparra have a ball in Fenway Park.
TOP: Tony Conigliaro   **RIGHT**: Johnny Damon

Talking Baseball

"My whole time in Boston, I gave everything I could—everything I knew I was about—on and off the field."

—*Nomar Garciaparra, on his devotion to the Red Sox*

"If I have my choice between a pennant and a Triple Crown, I'll take the pennant every time."

—*Carl Yastrzemski, on the joy of winning as a team*

"If there was ever a man born to be a hitter, it was me."
   —*Ted Williams, on why hitting came so naturally to him*

"My heart will always be with the Boston fans."
   —*Pedro Martinez, on his love for the city and the team*

"If I don't have good teammates, I don't win. If I don't have good teammates enjoying it with me, then it's no fun."
   —*Roger Clemens, on being part of a team*

LEFT: Nomar Garciaparra, one of the most beloved Red Sox.
ABOVE: Ted Williams, who was often called baseball's finest hitter.

For the Record

T he great Red Sox teams and players have left their marks on the record books. These are the "best of the best"…

Jackie Jensen

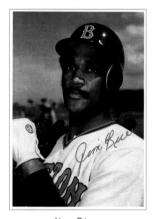

Jim Rice

RED SOX AWARD WINNERS

WINNER	AWARD	YEAR
Jimmie Foxx	Most Valuable Player	1938
Ted Williams	Most Valuable Player	1946
Ted Williams	Most Valuable Player	1949
Walt Dropo	Rookie of the Year	1950
Jackie Jensen	Most Valuable Player	1958
Don Schwall	Rookie of the Year	1961
Carl Yastrzemski	Most Valuable Player	1967
Jim Lonborg	Cy Young Award	1967
Carlton Fisk	Rookie of the Year	1972
Fred Lynn	Rookie of the Year	1975
Fred Lynn	Most Valuable Player	1975
Bill Campbell	Reliever of the Year	1977
Jim Rice	Most Valuable Player	1978
Roger Clemens	Most Valuable Player	1986
Roger Clemens	Cy Young Award	1986
John McNamara	Manager of the Year	1986
Roger Clemens	Cy Young Award	1987
Roger Clemens	Cy Young Award	1991
Mo Vaughn	Most Valuable Player	1995
Nomar Garciaparra	Rookie of the Year	1997
Tom Gordon	Reliever of the Year	1998
Pedro Martinez	Cy Young Award	1999
Jimy Williams	Manager of the Year	1999
Pedro Martinez	Cy Young Award	2000
Manny Ramirez	World Series Most Valuable Player	2004

RED SOX ACHIEVEMENTS

ACHIEVEMENT	YEAR
A.L. Pennant Winners	1903
World Series Champions	1903
A.L. Pennant Winners	1904
A.L. Pennant Winners	1912
World Series Champions	1912
A.L. Pennant Winners	1915
World Series Champions	1915
A.L. Pennant Winners	1916
World Series Champions	1916
A.L. Pennant Winners	1918
World Series Champions	1918
A.L. Pennant Winners	1946
A.L. Pennant Winners	1967
A.L. East Champions	1975
A.L. Pennant Winners	1975
A.L. East Champions	1986
A.L. Pennant Winners	1986
A.L. East Champions	1988
A.L. East Champions	1990
A.L. East Champions	1995
A.L. Pennant Winners	2004
World Series Champions	2004

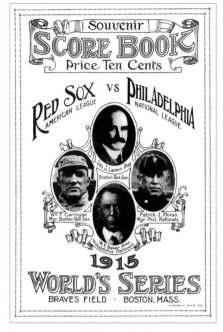

TOP: A scorecard from the 1915 World Series.
ABOVE: Roger Clemens, winner of the 1986 MVP and Cy Young awards.
LEFT: Jim Lonborg and Carl Yastrzemski return to Fenway Park with their trophies from 1967.

Pinpoints

The history of a baseball team is made up of many smaller stories. These stories take place all over the map—not just in the city a team calls "home." Match the push-pins on these maps to the Team Facts and you will begin to see the story of the Red Sox unfold!

TEAM FACTS

1   Boston, Massachusetts—*The Red Sox have played here since 1901.*

2   Bellows Falls, Vermont—*Carlton Fisk was born here.*

3   Anderson, South Carolina—*Jim Rice was born here.*

4   Hubbard, Texas—*Tris Speaker was born here.*

5   New Orleans, Louisiana—*Mel Parnell was born here.*

6   Aberdeen, South Dakota—*Terry Francona was born here.*

7   San Diego, California—*Ted Williams was born here.*

8   San Francisco, California—*Dom DiMaggio was born here.*

9   Portland, Oregon—*Johnny Pesky was born here.*

10   Anchorage, Alaska—*Curt Schilling was born here.*

11   Marianao, Cuba—*Luis Tiant was born here.*

12   Santo Domingo, Dominican Republic—
Manny Ramirez was born here.

Luis Tiant

Play Ball

Baseball is a game played between two teams over nine innings. Teams take one turn at bat and one turn in the field during each inning. A turn at bat ends when three outs are made. The batters on the hitting team try to reach base safely. The players on the fielding team try to prevent this from happening.

In baseball, the ball is controlled by the pitcher. The pitcher must throw the ball to the batter, who decides whether or not to swing at each pitch. If a batter swings and misses, it is a strike. If the batter lets a good pitch go by, it is also a strike. If the batter swings and the ball does not stay in fair territory (between the v-shaped lines that begin at home plate) it is called "foul," and is counted as a strike. If the pitcher throws three strikes, the batter is out. If the pitcher throws four bad pitches before that, the batter is awarded first base. This is called a base-on-balls, or "walk."

When the batter swings the bat and hits the ball, everyone springs into action. If a fielder catches a batted ball before it hits the ground, the batter is out. If a fielder scoops the ball off the ground and throws it to first base before the batter arrives, the batter is out. If the batter reaches first base safely, he is credited with a hit. A one-base hit is called a single, a two-base hit is called a double, a three-base hit is called a triple, and a four-base hit is called a home run.

Runners who reach base are only safe when they are touching one of the bases. If they are caught between the bases, the fielders can tag them with the ball and record an out.

A batter who is able to circle the bases and make it back to home plate before three outs are made is credited with a run scored. The team with the most runs after nine innings is the winner.

Anyone who has played baseball (or softball) knows that it can be a complicated game. Every player on the field has a job to do. Different players have different strengths and weaknesses. The pitchers, batters, and managers make hundreds of decisions every game. The more you play and watch baseball, the more "little things" you are likely to notice. The next time you are at a game, look for these plays:

PLAY LIST

DOUBLE PLAY—A play where the fielding team is able to make two outs on one batted ball. This usually happens when a runner is on first base, and the batter hits a ground ball to one of the infielders. The base runner is forced out at second base and the ball is then thrown to first base before the batter arrives.

HIT AND RUN—A play where the runner on first base sprints to second base while the pitcher is throwing the ball to the batter. When the second baseman or shortstop moves toward the base to wait for the catcher's throw, the batter tries to hit the ball to the place that the fielder has just left. If the batter swings and misses, the fielding team can tag the runner out.

INTENTIONAL WALK—A play when the pitcher throws four bad pitches on purpose, allowing the batter to walk to first base. This happens when the pitcher would much rather face the next batter—and is willing to risk putting a runner on base.

SACRIFICE BUNT—A play where the batter makes an out on purpose so that a teammate can move to the next base. On a bunt, the batter tries to "deaden" the pitch with the bat instead of swinging at it.

SHOESTRING CATCH—A play where an outfielder catches a short hit an inch or two above the ground, near the tops of his shoes. It is not easy to run as fast as you can and lower your glove without slowing down. It can be risky, too. If a fielder misses a shoestring catch, the ball might roll all the way to the fence.

Glossary

BASEBALL WORDS TO KNOW

ALL-STAR—A player who is selected to play in baseball's annual All-Star Game.

AMERICAN LEAGUE (A.L.)—One of the two major leagues. The A.L. began play in 1901.

AMERICAN LEAGUE CHAMPIONSHIP SERIES (ALCS)—The competition that has decided the American League pennant since 1969.

AT BAT—A turn hitting. "At Bats" are also a statistic that helps to measure how many times a player comes to the plate.

BREAKING BALLS—Pitches that move as they near home plate, such as a curveball, slider, or sinker.

CY YOUNG AWARD—The trophy given to each league's best pitcher each year.

FOUL POLE—One of the yellow poles in the outfield that mark the boundary between fair and foul territory. A foul pole is actually in fair territory—a ball that hits it is a home run.

INTENTIONAL WALKS—A statistic that measures the number of times a batter is walked on purpose.

MOST VALUABLE PLAYER (MVP)—An award given each year to each league's top player; an MVP is also selected for the World Series and All-Star Game.

NATIONAL LEAGUE (N.L.)—The older of the two major leagues. The N.L. began play in 1876.

PENNANT—A league championship. The term comes from the triangular flag awarded to each season's champion, beginning in the 1870s.

PINCH-HITTER—A player who is sent into the game to hit for a teammate.

PLAYOFFS—The games played after the regular season to determine which teams will advance to the World Series.

ROOKIE OF THE YEAR—An annual award given to each league's best first-year player.

RUNS BATTED IN (RBIs)—A statistic that measures the number of runners a batter drives home.

SHUT OUT—Did not allow an opponent to score. A game won in this way is called a "shutout."

SLUGGING AVERAGE—A statistic that helps to measure a hitter's power. Slugging average is calculated by dividing the number of total bases a batter has by his official times at bat.

TRIPLE CROWN—An honor given to a player who leads the league in home runs, batting average, and RBIs.

WILD CARD—A playoff spot reserved for the team with the best record, that has not won its division.

WORLD SERIES—The world championship series played between the the winners of the National League and American League.

OTHER WORDS TO KNOW

CELEBRITIES—People who are very famous.

CENTURY—A period of one hundred years.

DRAMA—A story that is exciting to watch as it unfolds.

EMPLOYEE—Someone who is paid to come to work each day.

EVAPORATE—Disappear, or turn into vapor.

FLANNEL—A soft wool or cotton material.

FRUSTRATED—Disappointed and puzzled.

LOGO—A company's official picture or symbol.

PURITANS—A religious group that settled in Massachusetts during the 1600s.

ROYALTY—A king or queen, or their relatives.

SYNTHETIC—Made in a laboratory, not in nature.

UNBEARABLE—Hard to put up with.

Places to Go

ON THE ROAD

FENWAY PARK
4 Yawkey Way
Boston, Massachusetts 02215
(877) 733-7699

NATIONAL BASEBALL HALL OF FAME AND MUSEUM
25 Main Street
Cooperstown, New York 13326
(888) 425-5633
www.baseballhalloffame.org

ON THE WEB

THE BOSTON RED SOX
- *to learn more about the Red Sox*

www.RedSox.com

MAJOR LEAGUE BASEBALL
- *to learn about all the major league teams*

www.mlb.com

MINOR LEAGUE BASEBALL
- *to learn more about the minor leagues*

www.minorleaguebaseball.com

ON THE BOOKSHELVES

To learn more about the sport of baseball, look for these books at your library or bookstore:

- Kelly, James. *Baseball.* New York, NY: DK, 2005.
- Jacobs, Greg. *The Everything Kids' Baseball Book.* Cincinnati, OH: Adams Media Corporation, 2006.
- Stewart, Mark and Kennedy, Mike. *Long Ball: The Legend and Lore of the Home Run.* Minneapolis, MN: Millbrook Press, 2006.

Index

The Team

MARK STEWART has written more than 25 books on baseball, and over 100 sports books for kids. He grew up in New York City during the 1960s rooting for the Yankees and Mets, and now takes his two daughters, Mariah and Rachel, to the same ball-parks. Mark comes from a family of writers. His grand-father was Sunday Editor of The *New York Times* and his mother was Articles Editor of *Ladies Home Journal* and *McCall's*. Mark has profiled hundreds of athletes over the last 20 years. He has also written several books about his native New York and New Jersey, his home today. Mark is a graduate of Duke University, with a degree in history. He lives with his daughters and wife, Sarah, overlooking Sandy Hook, NJ.

JAMES L. GATES, JR. has served as Library Director at the National Baseball Hall of Fame since 1995. He had previously served in academic libraries for almost fifteen years. He holds degrees from Belmont Abbey College, the University of Notre Dame and Indiana University. During his career Jim has authored several academic articles and has served in an editorial capacity on multiple book, magazine and museum publications, and he also serves as host for the Annual Cooperstown Symposium on Baseball and American Culture. He is an ardent Baltimore Orioles fan and enjoys watching baseball with his wife and two children.